Not So Simple

Observations on Poverty and People

First Edition

ISBN-13: 978-1985210745

ISBN-10: 1985210746

Not So Simple

Observations on Poverty and People

Brian Galetto

Table of Contents

II. Knowing the Neighbors

III. Planting Seeds for Change

Introduction

HERE'S A TYPICAL WEST COAST travel story. Fresh out of college, a twenty-two year old moves to California leaving everyone and everything he knew behind. He wanted to explore. He wanted to find himself. That's my story. I wanted to go somewhere where I was a nobody, where I could just be *Brian*.

It was at that point, when I left everything I knew, that I realized the power of community.

I ended up in the small Southern California town of Ojai working as a resident staff at a local boarding school. I adjusted well, keeping a low profile while trying to get my bearings. The following year I landed my first teaching gig and moved into a one-bedroom apartment on the fringe of downtown Ventura. Not long after I began writing *Not So Simple*. I found that writing could be a remedy for loneliness.

I did a lot of walking around Ventura. Same goes for Los Angeles and Santa Barbara. I saw a struggle I never knew existed. I knew the weather made it conducive to sleeping outside, but the problem of poverty felt deeper than that. When I explored Portland, San Francisco, Seattle and San Diego over my spring breaks and summer vacations, it became clear that my Southern California enclave was not the only place where homelessness and poverty were getting worse. That's when my curiosity kicked in.

As a teacher, I make my students focus on *why* and *how* when analyzing problems or scenarios. I applied the same criteria to thinking about poverty. *Why are there so many people struggling to get by? How can I help?* That's essentially how this project started. Then I quickly realized the answers were far from simple.

The more I studied and interacted with those affected by poverty, I began to understand how complicated this issue was. Language is powerful, so I wanted to use words to combat the narrative that all homeless were lazy and crazy. That's too generic, too simple. It's a crutch that at times can keep the public and politicians from helping.

Truth is, helping those in extreme poverty is a monumental challenge. That's *why* this problem has persisted. There's a multitude of roots that put people- and subsequently keep them- in poverty. Affordable housing, access to health care, education, and family ties/support networks all contribute to this, but they aren't the only reasons. There is no single story with poverty; homelessness has many faces.

At this point I had a better idea of *why* people were struggling. Then I began working towards answering the *how*.

That's when I started compiling stories I had gradually collected from people on the streets. Additionally I created a curriculum for my students which focused on developing empathy and compassion for others. Homelessness provided the perfect template for teaching young adults to be active agents of change in their communities. Which brings us to the goal of *Not So Simple*.

I wanted to create something that challenged how we see and interact with those living outside the margins of society. I wanted to amplify the voices of those living in an unfathomable reality. I wanted to hear their stories because I felt like everyone in our community deserves to be heard. I wanted to instill community not only in my classroom, but in the community I call home. Then I wanted to share this with other communities who were willing to listen. So that's what I did.

On my adventure out West I ended up finding *Brian*. I also ended up finding individuals like Frank, Matt, Amy, John, and countless others who you will hear from in the coming pages. These are people whose life stories were not as simple as they seemed. Full of joy, heartbreak, and uncertainty, their narratives center around human resilience, but also the human struggle; a struggle that is turning into a humanitarian crisis right before our eyes.

As a collective community I believe we can solve this issue. I believe that we can help alleviate poverty- and it starts by changing the way we see each other. It will take time. It will take patience. But we can make a difference. Those that are homeless are part of our society. We see them. They see us. This is where it starts- as individuals. Then it blossoms to the collective community; a community that is capable of change; united in the cause and commitment to creating a society that we can all be proud to call home.

I.

Welcome

to This

West Coast City

Persistence

Driving down Main Street
I see a man my age sorting through
Trash cans, collecting currency

Early morning
Even the sun isn't awake

A few hours later a lady
In her sixties
Sifts through rubbish
Revealing her social status

These situations aren't specific
To Ventura County
Nor are they only California's conundrum

Homelessness and poverty are seen
In major cities across the country

How can we help the homeless?

I'm so happy you asked

Real Talk

I would rather be hungry
Any day of the week than be
Invisible

Five minutes before I actively avoided
Eye contact with this man my age

In the next year,
Think of who could be out here

I see new faces every day
Males - females
Young and old
The streets don't discriminate

I stand here at 28 years old
And I can't afford to feed myself
Embarrassing, I know

His honesty and stream of consciousness
Sucked in the spectators
Waiting for the bus.
He was on a roll

I know what you're thinking
Don't give me your money
Who knows what I'll do
I don't blame you

He was saying what most were thinking
His dirt-caked hands were on the
Pulse of homelessness.
Sounding scared when he started
He now settled into his stage
The streets
His home.
The crowd stood still
Unsure of how to respond

I snagged the Cliff Bar I was saving
For my ride to LA.
He greeted me with gratitude
Grabbing my hand
Locked into my eyes,
He professed
I've been out here for six hours
And you're the third person to recognize me
Thank you

A few more people pitched in
And through that shift in energy
empathy emerged

I'd hug y'all if I didn't smell so bad!

We did it,
We created a human connection

Before this young man embarked back
Up the hills of Frisco
He had one more line
Of which to remind

The people you see out here
That's someone's
Son
Daughter
Brother
Sister

Invoking family
Especially lack of
Is a common concept on the streets

He hit his soapbox
Gathered necessary supplies to survive
& spoke of what it's like sleeping under the stars

Internally Compassionate

Five female students
Showed up to help the homeless
Which emphasized their proactiveness
Produced by empathy

We rolled around downtown
Looking for anyone in need

A few people looked like they could use it
But if you don't ask, it's hard to help

It's funny how
When you want to assist
Seek to make a difference
There's nothing there

Help doesn't work on a schedule
It's not convenient
It's just there
Whether you're ready or not

So don't be distraught, girls
The time will arise
When your community
Needs your energy and compassion
To create change
But remember that it's never about
You   or   Me
It's about helping
The whole
Where we all play our unique part
In piecing the puzzle together

Hung Out to Dry

2017 continues to bring bad news
There's been a 23% increase in homelessness
For the City of Angels.
People think the streets
Are for the drug fiends-
The lazy and crazy ones
Unwilling to work.
But people's eyes are opening
To that fact that those
Working like dogs
trying to provide
trying to survive
Are being hung out to dry

Rent control's not dead
But it's shallowly breathing
The city's rental market can get the resuscitation
It sorely needs if lawmakers can repeal
the monumental Costa-Hawkins Act of 1995
That took the cap off the max
of what you can charge
For a one family home or rental
Which means buildings built in the past twenty plus years
Can receive the protection needed
So that families aren't forking out
Over fifty percent of their income
and still unable to keep up
With the simple cost of being alive in Los Angeles.
If legislation can't cap the rent
and the ability to buy property
Remains impossible
for families making less than six figures
The number of those living on the streets
Will continue to climb
Which should make us wonder: *what's* the breaking point?
Will the market have to crash to get a correction?
2018 is bound to be worse

17

Fight On

Before bed
Reports on Twitter read
The blaze would be on the east end
By 1 or 2 am

Safe for a bit on the west side.
SIKE

The fire came four hours early
Surprise
But our downtown community
Made it out alive
Which is what counts

California now counts the single family homes
That were cremated without consent
But Mother Nature doesn't have to ask before she takes
And at the moment she's consumed close to 900 residences

We've done this to her
Now she's doing this to us
Regardless
There's no need to point fingers
Instead we can use them to pick up the broken pieces
Of a community
Of a state
Where the uncomfortable reality is that fire season is year round
Where people now realize the role of luck
In not having their house burned to the ground

Misfortune is a face that assists homelessness
In 2017 we saw Santa Rosa Santa Barbara Santa Paula & Ventura
Suffocate from the flames
Polluting the air
Pushing people to retreat
Pushing some to the streets

For the foreseeable future climate change and income inequality
Are the two biggest bears the Golden State will face
And they must continue to battle
Not giving up
Emulating the fire-fighters who fiercely fought the blaze
To protect the people
To protect the families
To protect the communities
From an inferno that is forcing Californians to consider the future of
This threatened Republic

Why Don't They Just Get a Job?

Everyone has a story
So for every story you share
Someone
Somewhere
Can relate

Tonight
It was Tatiana
With her fingers
Grasping my forearm
She thanked me
For thinking of the homeless

She had her own story
I come from Ukraine
And when I was younger my mother
And I took trains to Russia while she
Looked for work
We had no permanent home
which meant no permanent work
After interviews they wanted a number to call
But no phone means no job

Her words reminded me of the line
That people popularly use to describe their view
On homelessness
Why don't they just get a job?
I shared this with her

My mother tried,
Embarrassed,
She asked if she could contact them
In a few days to find out.
It rarely worked…

As our conversation closed
& I began to walk home

I kept thinking of Tatiana's story

To escape deep poverty you need a job
In order to get a job you need a place of contact
When that's not there
You rely on the willingness of a stranger to extend their hand
and subsequently change your narrative
All in the hopes of rewriting a story that is never, ever
as simple as it seems

Just Trying to Get By

HEY!

I jump from inside my kitchen half a block away
His anger is evident from here

Put that back!
Shut that lid!

It sounds like a cop about to arrest a suspect
I wonder:
What kind of valuables does this guy keep in his trash can?

I pop out of my chair and make my way outside
The energy is unavoidable

Before me stands an
Angry white man
Barking and berating
A short and stocky
Calm man with a dark tan

Looking defeated and dejected
He does as he's told
and slowly steps away from the trash can

He's not looking for trouble
He's just looking to get by
Which looks different for each of us

He gets on his bike and balances his bags
Brimming with crushed cans and
rides off
Searching for his next source of income
Anything
To help him make it
In this competitive and expensive
Coastal California city

Stuck in Time

The sun hadn't sucked the
nutrients from his face-
this means he's new to the avenues

He had the look in his eyes
Staring at the sidewalk
In a trance.
His brain was working
Yet struggling
Slowly   sputtering
Or maybe it was running faster
Than he could keep up.
He was stuck in his mind
While the moments trickled by

I've seen him four of the past five days
Then never again
His body is on the move
But his mind is far
far behind

West Coast Boom

Up and down the West Coast
There are less homes to house
A population that's projected to keep climbing

This has created states that are displaced

In 2017 the total headcount of those with no fixed address in
Washington Oregon and California
Hit 168,000.
Close to two-thirds of that population are people who are
Considered *unsheltered homeless*
Those who find refuge in
Vehicles - bus stations - under the stars
or protection of a bridge above
and concrete below

The tech boom has been fruitful for many
But now cities are struggling to find solutions
For how to help those being pushed out because of this success

State of Emergencies, typically reserved
For natural disasters
Have been issued in ten cities
Due to the homeless epidemic
Sweeping the warmer coast of our country

Amidst an affordable housing crisis
The American Dream has changed for people
Living in cities stretching from the Pacific Northwest
All the way down to the sunny San Diego coast.
People don't have to own a house
Realistically it's impossible for all to do so

We can deal with that

But as a society
the fact that we are unable to house people who have jobs

Points to a larger issue of inequality that we can no longer ignore
An issue that is deep rooted in   economics   race   and   education
An issue that we must work together to solve
if we want to save our cities
if we want to save our citizens

Soul Survival

His sign screamed
HUNGRY!
I had pizza for later
But later for me
Was present for him

Tough luck today?

You could say that
He muttered

Pizza?
A small nod
Led to a toss
Of my tinfoiled pieces
Of pepperoni pizza

A faint
Thanks
Escaped his lips

He looked battered and bruised
I'd seen him countless times
Same red hat
Same sad state

The streets can do that to a man
The mentality it must take to survive,
Convince your body not to give in
To hunger
To demons
To death

How would you keep your soul alive outside?

Walking Tired

Walking tired
Yet one foot still steps in front of the other

Bend of the knee
Looking like it might buckle

Shoulders slumped
Looking worn well beyond her years

I figured she was around fifty
But you never know when it comes to the concrete jungle
Too many variables
Life expectancy speeds up

She continues walking
With no direction
Black backpack
Blonde hair
Short in stature
Up and down
Back and around

Sit on the streets long enough
Consuming caffeine
& you'll see the lonesome travelers
With no place to call home
Always on the move

Walking tired
Up and down
Back and around

Locked Out

Heat wave in Phoenix
Put me inside Starbucks

Coffee
Lots of Coffee
Bathroom break

No punch code
Or purchase necessary
To use the pisser.
Standing there,
Processing this
It dawned on me:
Locks and codes let you know
Which communities have a problem
With perpetual poverty

For now
Phoenix is exempt from this

Checkmate

I lived in my car for a month

The young busboy's
matter of fact statement to his coworker
Showed he wasn't embarrassed
Knowing that in order to
maneuver the chessboard of real estate
In the Golden State,
Where the market is saturated with unrealistic rental prices,
His moves must be calculated

In order to buy some time
He lived in his ride
Which is a common play
For many West Coasters
Looking to get by

Man's Best Friend

With an abundance of energy
He pulled the tired knees
Of a man carrying
Two big black duffel bags

This poor pup doesn't know
The avenues he's so eagerly exploring
Will now be home for him and his master

Over time he will slow down
Realizing there is no rush
Or enough energy
To keep running at this pace

Just Hungry

No one was around
And lying on the ground
Was a cardboard sign
Freshly inscribed
With carefully colored
Bubble letters that read

Were just hungry

No need for an apostrophe
A symbol that shows
A grasp of grammar

I snatched the sign
Studied it
But the English teacher
In me didn't provide
The proper punctuation

Realistically the lack
Of this little mark
Between letters
Didn't misconstrue their message

Since grammar is
Useless in situations
Where one is
Just hungry

Psychology of Poverty

When psychologists study brains
of those who live in perpetual poverty
What they find are minds
That are as beat up as their bank accounts

The effects of reject
From jobs and housing
The weight of shame
When you have nothing to provide for your family
The savagery that results from circumstances
-Triggered from the simple need to eat-
Are hard to fathom for those who
Have always had the option to feast,
Always had the option to sleep
Under a roof instead of the stars
Always had something to give
Rather than receive.
There's a difference in self-esteem depending on
What side of the situation you find yourself on

A few years back Snickers ran a Super Bowl ad
    You're not you when you're hungry
A hungry white man named Mike
Turned into Betty White
Running routes
Getting knocked to the ground.
She walked back to the huddle
and right into smack talk from her teammates
Tempers flared
That was until she settled down and
Bit into the candy bar
Now Betty White morphed back into Mike
and everything returned to normalcy
Snickers Satisfies flashed across the screen to finish the story

The candy company used humor to hit on a reality that psychologist
A. H. Maslow made famous back in the forties
When he created his hierarchy of needs

People who have never experienced
Chronic hunger are apt to underestimate its effects
Hunger shows only one side to how poverty taxes the mind

When you're on the hunt for a house
When you're looking for a new gig to help you get by
When you're seeking to get out of the situation you're in
Only to be constantly turned down
Rejection begins to sting like the winter wind in the Midwest
One time turns to *two* which can spiral into *ten - twenty - thirty*
Times you've been declined
Persistence is part of success
But it's natural to wonder
When do you give up?
When do you throw in the towel?
When do you just accept the circumstances you're in?
Psychologists call these people
Exhausted settlers
Since they fought
Only to find they weren't what they- the employer or landlord-
were looking for

The human spirit
Is only so resilient
Poverty is painful
In the pockets
In the stomach
In the mind
In the eyes when you have to look at your kids
With nothing to give
Hopeless humans
Have to hustle however they can
Doing what they need to survive
Doing what they need to keep their family together
To keep food on the table
To keep their brain from accepting the despair
that poverty serves up
Day   after day   after day

The Heart and Art

Have some heart for the art, man!

The tourists by Santa Barbara's pier were unaware that
The sand sculptor was talking to them

Go ahead
Laugh
He says louder
But I'll tell you what I do,
I earn!

His tone now caught their attention

The man looks in his wallet
As his girlfriend grips his arm
I only have a ten

Without blinking the artist replies
I can break that

This Way, That Way

You could put arrows
Like this in every city
Homeless this way
Hipsters that way

Up and coming
Contrasted by
Long forgotten

Los Angeles spells it out

When you follow the sign
You see a society
pushed to the margins of the page

Skid Row
Alive
Thriving
Reminding
Angelinos
Of a struggle
That is far from over

Los Angeles, California

Santa Barbara, California

Santa Monica, California

Philadelphia, Pennsylvania

Los Angeles, California

Los Angeles, California

Ventura, California

Los Angeles, California

Boston, Massachusetts

44

Los Angeles, California

II.

Knowing

the

Neighbors

People on the Pier

The gates of Ventura's pier finally reopened
El Niño gave it a good shot
But like any seasoned fighter
It took its punches
and continued to stand tall

I walk the half-mile stretch of downtown's backyard
Listening to the lull of the waves
Until chatter from the fishermen
Reel me in

I could annihilate a 6x6 with animal fries
Standing there
Tall and slender
He looks in need of a hearty meal
But his words were wishful

I'm ready to eat!
Remarks his friend
Ready, yet like his buddy
Hopeful but helpless

For the two of them
The dreams of
In-N-Out might as well
Be pie in the sky

Their longing for food makes fishing
Much more important,
Maybe even essential
for survival

The fish don't bite that night
and the wind isn't the only cold hard truth
That begins to settle in

Public Knowledge

If you want a sense of
What poverty looks like in any city
Head to the public library,
A building constructed upon
The ideology that everyone in the community-
Regardless of skin tone and income,
Should have equal access to resources
& knowledge that the brain so desperately craves

West Coast libraries prove pivotal
To those with
No home to charge phones
No computer to look for jobs and housing
No access to ideas other than their own

This is a safe space that provides temporary relief from the streets

In Seattle I saw
People passed out
On tables
While others rifled
Through magazines

In Portland
I witnessed a man washing
His shirt in the bathroom sink

In Los Angeles,
Where the public library serves
the largest pool of residents,
I watched a man brush his teeth
While a stroller was parked in the stall.
I walked through the second and third floors
Which were brimming with community tables
Packed with people from all parts of the city.
The police stroll through
Looking for sleepers,

Looking for something…
Letting it be known
That if you aren't trying to stimulate your mind
Then you're out of time

Libraries are little communities
When we walk through those doors
Our differences dissipate
Yes
Some smell more than others
Some have extra baggage they can't let go of
But we enter to activate the brain
To get lost in a story
That can provide hope
Needed
to get through
Another day
Another night
Reminding us through the written word
Not to give up
Reminding us through art that we are
Better
when the community comes together
Reminding us with each punch of the keyboard
Or each stroke of the pen
That the public library
& the public are intertwined
Our stories
Merging if only for a moment
At a building
Where equality and equal access
Is & forever will be
For everyone in the community

Family Fun

There they were
A family of four
Walking State Street
On a quintessential Santa Barbara afternoon

Brothers chasing each other
Playing with the crosswalk buttons
On every corner

They'd run around their mother
Who pushed a cart full of cans
Smiling and laughing
Like they were exploring
Disneyland

Poverty hasn't robbed them
Of their childlike wonder

Kids find fun for free
All while mom and pops
Find cans to keep their family afloat

Small Gestures

She was looking the other way
But I called to her anyway

Excuse me miss
As I held out my hand

She could care less
What I handed her

You called me miss,
Not ma'am

With a warm smile
She touches my hand
You made my day

Flattery is for everyone

Kids in Poverty

Each year
close to 1.5 million students
experience homelessness
Sadly
This number continues to rise
While federal funding remains flat

This is a part of poverty
most don't see

It is not a choice for these children
They know nothing else
They were born into this
The inadequate access to
Food   Shelter   and   Safety
Is something they are accustomed to

For all the instability, there is one stabilizer:
School

For everyone outside
Asking for help
Was once a student

It's possible those we see on the streets
grew up in poverty
This is unknown to us
Since their signs never say
I grew up in a broken home
Poor and with only one parent
I'm a product of my environment
I needed help then
And I need help now

As seeds of poverty are sewn
from a young age
They begin to blossom based

off what they were fed,
So when you mix the instability above
With underfunded classrooms
It doesn't require much math to see how students go from
Classrooms to
Courtrooms
To street corners
Or hospital beds

Mayhem in the Mind

Please God, end this for us
Please God, blessed be in your name

It's not often you get an inside look at a
Mind that's damaged and disturbed,
But walking over the footbridge
connecting the edge of downtown to the beach
I found a backpack rifled through,
Ideas discarded.
Impossible to know the culprit
Yet what was clear from her writing
Was her struggle

Thoughts
written in beautifully punctuated prose
Her cursive contained a multitude of references to religion
All in an attempt to be rescued from the world she's in
Full of sin
Now she's sunk into depression

I'm begging
please God
Please
Kill me
And take me from my misery
For four years
Come May 26th
I no longer exist
Going through toil
Torment and treason

Four years
struggling
with a lingering experience
that continuously
eats at her sanity
Like a small leak that drips daily

and finally bursts through

Her pain's been pent up
And then put on paper.
Writing as a release valve-
A therapy I endorse

With no idea who she is or where she lives
I too talk to God
and send her a prayer
Through a poem

Can You Blame Me?

How can I get a meal out here?

An honest question
Delivered in an
Aggressive manner
to no one in particular

Unlocking my bike
I stopped
Paused
and decided to
Engage

Any luck today?
I knew the answer
But this question gives me a sense of
The individual
In front of me

Pessimist

He wasn't expecting me to
Acknowledge him

His mannerisms immediately changed
Looking down at the curb
He muttered a
No, not really

He held his hand
and in moving his fingers
Revealed a freshly formed
Gash around his knuckles

What happened to you?

He could tell I cared

I got mad
Cop woke me up
I was drunk
He caught me off guard-
I got angry
Can you blame me?

He sounded sorry
But I wasn't there to pass judgment
Or validate any opinion

I could only think of whether or not
I wanted to share my fish tacos

The more we talked
The more anxious he got

Luckily we had some space
Separating us on the sidewalk

He continued talking
I've been homeless a few weeks...

Hopefully he realizes that
anger
Won't get him any meals
Yet asking for help isn't easy
It bruises the ego

Wishing him well
I hopped on my bike and although
I didn't share my meal with him
We shared a conversation

and he seemed grateful for that

Calling Home

Fire engines are still racing through the streets
Sirens that haven't slept in weeks
Yelling
Telling
Us that structures are still burning
People are still hurting
and will be well after the Thomas fire is finished

For over five-hundred families in Ventura
Home is no longer a house
Home is now a memory
Home is no longer a space
It's the city or place
Where memories were made
First dates,
Graduate,
Remember that time when...

Home is now *generic*
The specific spot where people once slept is gone
Ever since the largest fire in California's history
Called Ventura and Santa Barbara County
Home

Impostor

I saw her
Sitting in front of the pub
Looking helpless
Asking for money

Her face still looked fresh
The streets hadn't
Taken its toll yet

Fast forward

I saw her
Leaving downtown
In a red jeep
Driving past the pub
She posted up in front of

I saw her
Then see why
People are hesitant to help the homeless

An impostor
Who ruins it for the rest

Frank Who Could Fly

He didn't look like
Most men I met
On the streets

He was well dressed
Nicer than me
Actually

But his feet were swollen
His body looked worn
and he wore a red pack
On his back

Catching me off guard
He extends his hand

I hesitate

Frank he says
Aw what the hell, I think
Brian
as our palms push together

Rambling from the get go
He spoke of his grandfather
Who he described as 98 years young

I had no idea what he was talking about
It was coherent
But strange
However I didn't misconstrue his next message
This is my home
As he firmly placed his foot on the pier

He talked about doing drugs
Being out of the house for eight to nine months
and having a family with kids

I couldn't separate the real from the fake

He spoke of God
being chosen
and battling demons;
He felt singled out

Pointing to the parking structure
He matter-of-factly-stated
I thought of jumping off that building
and seeing if I could fly.
I did it when I was a kid
Now I have plates in my leg

He takes drugs for pain
and to 'manage'
He didn't say what
I'm guessing his mind

Mentally ill
But not too far gone
Far as I could tell

He remembered my name
When the conversation came to a close

It was nice meeting you, Brian
The feeling was mutual

Frank was lost in a sea of thoughts
Looking for someone to swim with
As he rambled from one wave to another
I decided to catch a few rides with him
Before it was time to head back to shore

Fortunate 500

Morning bus
Headed to headquarters
Fortunate people
Working for major
Fortune 500 companies

The disparity
In our economy
Won't blind those
Who board the bus
From poverty

Those that share
The same biology
Yet lack technology
Look on as luxurious
Shuttle busses brimming
With America's finest
Minds make their way
To the valley of riches

Google and
Facebook
Possess personal information
From almost everyone
In the U S of A
They program people
To think and feel
But the people
Whose information
They lack are left out

Those long stares
In the morning
Looking at one another
Even if
Separated by glass
From the windows

From their phones
Have the capacity to
Create a human connection
If enough interest
Is sparked

I wonder,
What role,
What obligation,
Do these tech giants
have in helping out those
Who are now locked out of a housing market?
A market in the Bay that is buckling
In part due to the money being pumped in from Silicon Valley
Because of the ever increasing role technology plays
For people in their daily life

For all the power that
Google and Facebook possess
They should propose solutions to fix an issue
That their employees see
Every day
As they board the bus
To headquarters
Where the goal is always
Keep them hooked
Keep them connected
Keep them engaged
Not in real life
But online
Where they can't see the poor

Light Years

Sometimes I speed through lights
Not wanting to get stuck at street corners

Look left
Look right
Despair is out tonight

With nothing to give I feel helpless
Even though I'm not the one who's homeless

The light is still red and
Avoiding his eyes is the only thing on my mind

Finally I push past my discomfort and
Flash a peace sign packaged with a solemn nod

Green means go
Driving away the man is out of sight
But in Southern California
Never out of mind

Next corner
New person
Same idea

Anything helps
Thank you
God Bless

Questions

Questions help fill in the gap
Of what we don't know
but desire to learn

Poverty breeds more questions than answers

It typically takes many questions
Coupled with an active listening stance
To figure out
Why or how
Someone ended up
In deep poverty
and how they get by
Day after day

If you could ask any question
What would you choose?
A *why?*
How?
What?
Now?
When?
Where?
or *who?*

What [pronoun] *asking for information specifying something*
What did you want to be when you grew up?
What's your biggest regret?
What's the most important thing you need living outside?

How [adverb] *in what way or manner*
How would you describe your childhood?
How can I help you?
How would you describe your current situation?

When [adverb] *at what time*
When do you feel loneliest?

When is the last time you had a room that locked?
When is the last time you talked to your family?

Where [adverb] *in or to what place or position*
Where is the safest place for you to stay?
Where do you go when you're sick?
Where do you usually sleep?

Why [adverb] *for what reason or purpose*
Why do some people prefer living outside?
Why does the homeless population continue to grow?
Why do those who live on the streets struggle to leave?

Who [pronoun] *what or which person or people*
Who do you try and avoid?
Who do you consider family?
Who do you go to when you need help?

With a complex topic like poverty
answers are intricate
Asking questions allows others to tell their story
All while bringing
the listener and speaker
Closer to understanding each other

Death in the Dark

In the early hours of morning
A man was stabbed
Again
Again and
Again

They found his homeless body
Slumped over at the bus stop
Stationed across from the funeral home

Anger is on the streets
and when you're homeless with no place to hide
You are subject to the blind rage
That runs rampant at night

Categorized

I
We
You
are part of a compassionate community
Comprised of misguided charitable givers

Last night I heard that local Venturans were hurting more than
helping
Enablers
because groups passed out food and clothes for those who asked for
help

As I sat in on the Pierpont Community Council meeting
A knowledgeable man before us passionately broke down
a problem he's spent his professional life trying to manage

He placed people in poverty within three categories:
The *have nots* or working poor
The *can nots* or those who are physically or mentally unable to work
The *will nots* or those who won't work; the ones we've been
enabling

The question he posed and
the one California is currently trying to figure out
Is how to deal with those who fall into the *will not* category

By placing people in categories he's setting up a structure
To help identify who wants   who needs   and   who doesn't desire
help

He knew he was in for an onslaught of questions by a
Predominantly old and Caucasian population
Most questions accounted to people persecuting the poor instead of
trying to better understand the issue
and seek possible solutions.
It's fair to be frustrated
But complaining without a course of action
Doesn't accomplish much

Armed with knowledge
he handled each question with wit and a hefty dose of logic

"Why can't you lock them up?"
For what? Standing around?
"They're high! I've seen them dealing drugs"
Then call the cops and then stay around and wait for them to arrive
Why can't you get them out of here?"
Where do you want them to go?

The solutions to this epidemic are far from simple
Ventura has no day services and only 22 shelter beds
There is no profit margin for hospitals to house the mentally ill.
He saved his most poignant point for last,
Forcing Pierpont, Ventura, and California residents to take a long
look in the mirror
If they want to move towards a solution

Where do you want them to go? None of you want them near you.
Every time an affordable or low housing project is put to the public,
It doesn't pass.
It's too close to my church,
too close to my house,
too close to where I shop.

His passion was palpable to everyone who was truly listening.
I wish he had a mic to amplify his voice to the 39 million inhabitants
of the Golden State,
To highlight that people working in public services are fighting for
change but because of the pushback from people in the community,
plus local government issues,
little to nothing happens

He is close to retirement
Tired and frustrated he stated his main point without saying it:
If we want to truly help ease poverty,
we must change how we engage with and view
those that are affected by it

One Block

Walking home
Late Los Angeles night in November

On one long Downtown block
I ran into three stories surrounding
homelessness

The first was an elderly lady at the corner
She was speaking,
Lamenting,
Looking for anyone who would listen.
She made eye contact with
A younger woman

With a where-did-it-all-go-wrong tone
she stated that she was homeless
and when the young girl heard this sad sound
she offered a helping hand
But where to even go?
the older lady asked.
Good question
Giving needs some semblance of cohesion
Planning
Spur of the moment is a challenge.
But this young lady proved that people *are* willing to help strangers
When called upon

In the middle of the block a small boy walked with his
young parents
His dad stealthily hawked cans out of the trash
and tossed them into the shopping cart his wife pushed
on Black Friday.
Those cans could buy food and heat
which are presents those of us outside of poverty take for granted

On the opposite end of the corner from where this story started

A young man was decking out an alternative sign to back up his current colorful and creatively designed piece of cardboard which underscores how he could be a graphic designer working to appeal to people for help even though most of those who pass him by just graze his sign since this sight is nothing new and this night in Los Angeles was no different

Postgame Sadness

Sick to my stomach
That's how I felt
As my neighbor and I
Drove along the foothills of
Ventura

Inside the Clearpoint housing tract it's
A scene of what used to be

Rubble   ash   chimney
House
Rubble   ash   chimney
House
Rubble   ash   chimney
House

The devil played a twisted game of hopscotch
Ruining the American Dream for families along the way

KTLA news vans were there to cover the aftermath
Like sideline reporters on a postgame show
No one wanted to watch
But we stayed glued to the tube
Wanting to know where the devil was playing next

Beginning

Young bulls
Busting their way through Santa Barbara
On their four-wheel boards.
They have a shtick
and as a showman myself
I respect their act.
The first couple passed on their pitch
But his buddy egged them on
He had a good line, though, right?!
He wanted to validate his friend's words.
The couple did not disagree
But gave no money.
Riding along
The headliner screamed
Arrest the wind!
To the security guard stationed on the
Red brick sidewalk.
Calling shots from the streets,
This could be the beginning
of a downward spiral that
would make his stage
A permanent fixture.
Home. Sweet. Home.
As the twenty-some-year-old boys circled back
They finally found someone
Who folded from their energy
and reluctantly passed a buck.
Mental illness
Has many roots
Perpetuated by drugs
Starting young
Quickly turns old
Because when you lose your wit
There goes your shtick

Vision Blurred

My name is Matt Wilkerson and I'm from Wyoming
I'm celebrating my birthday this month

Throughout our brief interaction he repeated this line three times

With one eye glassy and protruding from his socket
Who knows what this man's seen.
I know what he hasn't seen
Healthcare

A transplant
California refugee
Who moved southwest
Searching for something different

He was not alone on his journey
Two men,
Friends,
Acted as guardians
For Matt Wilkerson from Wyoming
Who has a birthday this month

Still Alive

I see the same man
Standing by Sanjon
His old body bounces
Between Seaward and Harbor Blvd-
The streets that harbor those seeking help

You can't call him lazy
I'd say strategic
Because rain or shine
He's out there
Looking for work
Looking for food
Looking for help
Looking into your eyes
and after all these years he's still alive
Living off kindness

Demanding Attention

I walk the train tracks
Searching for the perfect perspective.
Photography can put you in
Unique positions

I crouch
Balance my frame
But before I shoot
I'm startled by someone's voice

Ten feet from me,
A man lays
Nestled against a white barricade

The overhead protection
Of the overpass
Keeps him dry.
No one will find him here
Unless they too are seeking
Refuge from the rain

Huddled up in his camouflage jacket
Hood covering his eyes
He's struggling to sleep

Anger spews from his lips.
The demons demand his attention

Bastard [yell-grunt]
why would you…[huffing] I told you…
His anger fueled rant
Was directed towards someone he couldn't see

Later that night
while lying in bed
My mind runs
But not as fast as his

I couldn't help but think
Of his voice
The pent up anger and agitation

The true picture of mental illness
a camera can't catch

San Diego, California

Los Angeles, California

Ventura, California

Los Angeles, California

Philadelphia, Pennsylvania

Santa Barbara, California

Berkeley, California

Ventura, California

San Diego, California

Ventura, California

III.

Planting

Seeds

For

Change

Bombs Bursting at Night

oh say can you see
the man
by the dawn's early light
Sitting on the pavement
what so proudly we hailed
Vietnam Vet cap on
at the twilight's last gleaming
Accepting anything you have to offer

In the land of the free and the home of the brave
Our veterans are heralded as heroes on Veterans Day.
When the day's over, those feelings fade
and celebrating their sacrifice
turns to annoyance as
Patriots in the truest sense
sit outside of storefronts,
Post up in public parks,
and struggle to make a life
After the war.
Because of bombs bursting in the air
PTSD is still there-
So is substance abuse.
This common coping method highlights
the perilous fight that is just beginning for some
as they settle into life under the bright stars
strapped with their broad bags and nowhere to go

Walk around any major city
In the land of the free and home of the brave
and you'll see that our flag is still there
flying high above
Veterans asking for help
From their country
From the citizens
From all of those who
Sing the Star Spangled Banner

Selling Hope

Would you like to buy _____?
Sitting on the corner
She was selling something

I wasn't interested.
A nod and excuse flow from my mouth

I keep walking.
Five minutes later....
Damnit!
I was going the wrong way

As I work my way back I see her again
This time I'm ready to listen

Whatchu selling?
Newspapers
About what?
Homelessness

Pointing to her papers she says,
if you stay clean
off drugs and away from booze
you can make some money selling papers
and get back on your feet

Sold
I bought a few

It was a wet day in the city of Brotherly Love
and coupled with the cold
I admired her willingness to fight for a better life

She's struggled on the streets
but now
she's getting back on her feet

Future Activist

After school
She walked into my classroom
Wanting to talk about the homeless

A former student
Spoke fiercely about empathy
I tell my friends
How would you feel living like that?
Rather 'would' you feel?
Do you know what it would be like living outside?
Can you try putting yourself in their shoes?

Her energy was felt with each word-
A future activist indeed

Asking questions is at the heart of this social emotion
and this teenager
Who is trying to understand herself
Her place in society
Has curiosity
Care
and a passion to share
With others
Even if it's a bit rough around the edges
At the moment

Curriculum of Life

My coworker told me our dorm students
Slept at the homeless shelter last night

The Thomas Fire taught them something I never could

In my classroom
We turned October into #Socktober
Stocking up on socks and toiletries to pass off to homeless shelters
We watched Soulpancake's YouTube series
called *Stories from the Streets* & studied individual people, trying to
empathize with each story
We read "Why the Poor Stay Poor"
Which in the most basic sense explains the economics of poverty
& what one or two bad breaks can do to you

Experience is our best teacher

For these students
I hope this is the closest they get to being homeless
And for all the people who were displaced from the fire,
Whether sleeping in shelters or holed up in hotels,
I hope they remember all of the emotions from this experience
Since exposure to stepping in shoes other than their own lays the
foundation for empathy

Facts

Poetry doesn't have to rhyme
California is the most populous state

Poetry is the human struggle
California has a housing crisis highlighted by a lack of affordable housing

Poetry reflects reality
There are only four metropolitan areas in the United States where more than half of the homes are priced above 500,000: San Jose, San Francisco, Los Angeles/Orange County, and San Diego

Poetry doesn't have to rhyme
At 66.4%, California leads the nation in unsheltered homeless

Poetry is the human struggle
Homelessness in CA grew by 2.1% in 2016, while the national average decreased by 2.6%

Poetry reflects reality
California has the country's highest poverty rate at 20.4%

Cardboard Communication

There is no escaping people in poverty
Especially in Southern California

People of all ages and aspects of life
Walk the streets they call home

The weather is typically right at night
No snow or much precipitation
Fortunately for them
Unfortunate for the environment

Strolling the streets
The medium for communication runs through cardboard
Need supplies
Hungry
Anything helps

Anything does help
Even if I've been turned down when
Trying to lend a helping hand.
It's natural
Sometimes people don't want what you're sellin'
Or in this case
Givin'

Yet communication changes
When your eyes graze the cardboard

A cautious, sometimes shameful
Sound emanates from their lips
Excuse me, can you spare some change?

This is the challenge
I believe deep down that people want to help
Naturally it's in us

But when help has gone from *anything* to *currency*

people are put in precarious positions

What to do?
Maybe
Instead of blowing by
pretending not to hear
we slow down
Make eye contact,
perhaps an apology leaps from our lips
Not because we did something wrong
but because we can't provide the type of help they need

What we can do is provide validation
that they are indeed human
Beggars have
a heartbeat
favorite movie
pulse
and a wanting to be recognized
rather than ignored

A few blocks later the same situation unfolds

Perseverance and compassion for others is essential
To creating conscious communities

Don't give up
On either end
Because at the end of the day
We all need each other

Luck of the Landlord

For most people over the past century
Spending 30% of your income on housing was appropriate

Modest increases were expected
Except now rent rises faster
Than the pace of one's paycheck

In 2017 it's not irrational to spend half your income on housing

If we look to the landlord,
The role that luck plays
When searching for somewhere to live
Can't be overemphasized

If you find a property owner
Who has a moral compass
When it comes to making money,
Valuing the tenants
Who put their hard earned cash
in his or her account monthly,
Then the renter will be in a practical position

If your proprietor
Understands and values the importance
Of a functioning society's structure
Then when they rent they won't price gouge for the sole purpose of
Putting more money in their pocket

On the flipside, when your luck runs dry
and your slumlord thinks of people as pawns,
Pitting them against each other ,
Squeezing out their desperation and eagerness
Because housing isn't an optional commodity,
The game becomes stacked against the tenants

The allure of disproportionately profiting off of people
You don't personally know is a tactic

Bad Businesses utilize
And when there are enough of these businesses out there
The bank accounts of the vulnerable run as dry
As a Los Angeles water reservoir

Landlords who exploit and extract
What they can
Not what they should
Have hurt communities throughout the country-
Especially considering the constant shuffle of people
Moving because they are unable to afford their current residence.
But that's part of the game
When the former leaves the future pays more
Which means the uphill climb of those looking
to pull themselves out of poverty
gets steeper and steeper,
More unattainable each day

Since it's damn near impossible
for people in poverty to buy property
The cyclical nature of the housing market will allow for
money to forever flow into the pockets
Of the affluent
Residual income will reside in their family
For as long as the building is in their name
and we know the name of this game
We've played Monopoly before
One building typically turns to two
Two to four
For as long as rent remains high
Then the properties will keep piling up.
The rich get richer
While the poor are left to pick off the scrap heap.
Trump's Tax Cuts and Jobs Act bill highlights this

Unfortunately it's luck of the draw
Since there aren't enough regulations to keep
Property owners from pricing properties however they like.
It sucks to say but until the government steps up we're stuck with a
young adult dystopian novel phrase: *May luck be ever in your favor*

Street Parking

Heard the news on my way to school
Santa Barbara banned RVs from parking on their streets
Agitated, I thought this was a veiled attempt
to cover the contempt of the homeowning city's residents
Who feel that those who can't afford
the luxury of living on a plot of land
On the pristine coast of Southern California
Should be banned

But before I bury this city with words
I found that they were providing structured parking lots
For the homeless with services to serve
Those looking for help,
Those who hope to not always live on wheels

They're providing a form of rehabilitation for
their less than lucky residents.
That's reassuring.

Like any pressing problem that's tough to solve
Santa Barbara proposed a possible solution
For a conundrum where it's almost impossible
to please everyone.

For that
I'll give an encouraging clap
Then turn back
to LA and ask
Whatchu got?

What We Don't See

Mental illness
Doesn't stick out
Or elicit sympathy
The way physical or visible
Ailments tend to

Broken arm?
The thought of a bone protruding
From one's skin
Can cause us to cringe
Resulting from what our brain
Conjured up

But soon they'll be patched up
fit with a sling
and back to society

When we see them
We'll ask how it happened
and how we can help
Let me grab that door
Or *I'll grab those groceries for you*
Carry your backpack even

So why do we fail to assist
Or feel for
The body that does not look broken?
Why is it that the only thing we pass towards the mentally ill is
judgment?

Choices

Is this book of poetry worth it?
People have their own problems
Why should they care about others?
Especially the homeless

They're *all*
a bunch of bums,
boozing and cruising through life
looking for handouts from others

I've heard that from kids,
Friends my age,
Even adults
Who should know that life is never
As simple as it seems

They look at me like *I'm* the crazy one
and maybe I am
But if crazy is categorized
as caring for the marginalized
Then count me in

Cruising to the coffee shop
Doubting my intentions
I see firsthand why we must care

There's a man in the middle of the street
Belt around his neck
Looking dazed and confused
He nods to me

A car honks its horn
Motioning him to move
He says nothing
Stares at them
Then shuffles his feet forward

Ten minutes later a lady walks down Main
Slowly stepping sideways
Like she's playing the childhood game
Hot lava
She stops
Kneels and
Pops a white substance from the street
Into her teeth-
Stillness.
Then she too moves

Different genders
Different ages
Same predicament
There are members of our community out there
Who need us to ask
Not just *how* can we help
But simply *can we* help?
Since we can only assist
Those who are ultimately willing to help themselves

The decision is theirs
Even if they sometimes make the wrong one

Chapter 3

Midtown Ventura
Where the liquor stores
suck in the helpless every other block

With blankets in hand
and everything he owned
packed on his back
He began to walk my way
As I sat outside the laundromat

Can you spare some cents?

Clever way to say it

I'm a terrible liar.
Caught in a conundrum,
I took two quarters from my pocket
My senses said no
but my body begrudgingly gave in

I almost asked how he'd spend it
Yet since I'm going to give
My money is now his

Before he left
I hit him with a 'how's it hanging?'
Instead of a 'how ya doing?'
I too could be clever with my words
Because I wanted a genuine response

He went into weather, which is generic
But he experiences it more than most
since his home is everywhere and nowhere at the same time

It's hot man!
I think the weather is bipolar

Interesting way to describe it

Maybe his mind has experience

One more minute then he's moved on

Cautiously crossing the street,
he steps into a liquor store

This broad brush that people use to paint a picture of homelessness
is not always accurate.
What was accurate is that
Today
This man proved that his story includes substance abuse
But this is only one chapter of his story
and his story is different from my story
Or your story
Or any story

Speak Up

Have you ever been so lonely
that you speak
just to remind yourself
you have a voice?

Close to Capacity

Sitting inside I heard the Santa Ana winds
Whipping violently
Pushing the palms around,
Coupled with the pitter patter of rain
This was Mother Nature speaking up
For all to hear
For all to feel
Especially when you have no
Place to call home

I thought of Matt Wilkerson from Wyoming
Then the older man who seeks refuge on Harbor Blvd
The people who post up in front of In-N-Out
Those who are scattered throughout Plaza Park
Veterans who were trained to deal with Mother Nature

Constant California sunshine means
People don't always need
to worry about the weather
But the wet winter of 2016,
Where La Niña came with constant rain,
put a dent in the drought
and throughout
California
The number of homeless rose
Like the water reservoirs

close to capacity
ready to burst

In the Face of Anger

Dealing with those who have a mental illness
Takes a certain kind of stillness
A mentality made up of
Kindness
Patience
and a persistent reminder to try and understand
So you can withstand
Sudden emotional outbursts
Stemming from only-they-know

I've seen one-on-one situations play out before me
In coffee shops
street corners
and on the Amtrak

It starts more or less the same
The individual is
Subdued
Staring, stewing about something
Then without the slightest warning
SNAP
Anger and agitation are expressed
and now it's time for the test

As an onlooker I watch for three things:
Can the individual(s) in the vicinity keep calm?
Can the person(s) engaged handle the staring eyes around them?
Can they de-escalate the situation?

As the interaction unfolds
The ones who have success
Stay the same
Emotionally intelligent individuals,
they are unwavered by the anger or
obscenities screamed-
They are committed to caring
Knowing that this is part of the game

That is actively playing out the same way
across the country

This mentality is made up of mental exercise
To strengthen one's emotional response.
Practicing isn't always pretty because
Sometimes no matter how calm
and careful you are
You still can't help
But by trying we're creating a culture of compassion
and over time we can change the perception
Of how we interact with
and see those who
suffer from a mental illness

A Natural Disaster

The distinctions of what a 'once in a hundred year' storm
truly means
In the age of climate change has changed

Catastrophic storms are unfortunately the new norm
And Hurricane Harvey and Irene highlighted
another crack in society
One that was brought up but brushed under the rug during Katrina:
People in poverty are the most vulnerable and hardest hit
When Mother Nature slams her fists

To be clear
Everyone suffered-
The storms didn't just pick on the poor.
However when Harvey finally hit Houston
and the entire city struggled with record level floods
The eight counties that received the bulk of the devastation
Were those where less than 20% of families had flood protection.

This wasn't by accident

Cities are socially structured to keep the poor and minorities
confined to certain sectors
These are the undesirable areas with
insufficient infrastructure for drainage
These are the areas closest to industrial pollution
when power plants are suddenly shut down

Then evacuate, they say. Get out of town before it's too late.
Yet when storms strike close to the first of the month
Like Hurricane Irma did
Escaping isn't so easy.
In Miami Dade County
Where half a mil, or ⅙ of the population
live below the poverty line
Leaving is a challenge
It costs money

And when you've spent your check on rent gas & electricity
There's no convenience of cash lying around
Realistically you run the risk that you may drown
So when you can't afford to get out of town
you hunker down and hope for the best
hope
that you're not homeless once the storm's relentless wrath
Has passed

And then you're in the aftermath
Where if you work for an hourly wage, you don't get paid
For piecing your life back together.

Pray for Food

Two men
Tatted up
Stand waiting for
Their prayer group

While waiting
I heard
Lots of talk about
The Lord Almighty

At the depths of their despair
These former felons found something in Jesus

Then the moment of truth arrived
In the form of an elderly homeless man asking for help

What Would Jesus Do?

Politely and concisely
They led him astray
'If you pray,
We'll send food your way!'

Prayers don't fix the rumbling in his stomach
But now they had his ear
Because soon he'd have his grub

Grabbing his hands
Holding them tight
With eyes closed
They deliver words from above
A long prayer filled with the typical buzzwords
Jesus
    Saves
      Repent
        Sins
So you can get out of this life you're in

Amen

The prayer was over and now he was lickin' his lips
Ready to bite into whatever they offer

He holds out his hands
Like a beggar from the Bible
and receives a voucher for Jack in the Box

Confused
He just stares
at them
Then the voucher
He can't eat this
With no means of transportation
How could he cash in?
The two men couldn't even communicate the location

Standing at Horton Square
in San Diego
they wanted to help
But these men of the Lord were only armed with prayer
and they quickly found out that even with good intentions
and God by their side
It's hard to help the homeless

Tell Me I'm Pretty

This 20-some-year-old
Former Miss America
Made a poignant point
To everyone listening at a school-wide assembly:
Visually appealing people
Are oftentimes spared from
Living outside

I was homeless,
But I'm pretty
So I always had a couch to sleep on

A smug look spread across her face
As she finished her sentence

Her statement accentuated another face of poverty
One that underscores what wealth looks like

If you're pretty you've got currency
not in the physical form
but in the facial or physique of your body
Which can be cashed in whenever you need a place to crash

Change-ing

Lines were long
Near the 101 as I
waited for gas

Off to the side
A man and his dog
Sit with their sign
Anything will help

This view was nothing new
But I was out of money
and forgot to bring more food

How can I help?

Before I could finish my thought
A woman worked her way to my window

Excuse me sir
Could you spare some change?

I *could,* but I didn't want to
I avidly avoid giving money

It's Ok if you can't
Her words sounded sadder
Than the state of her sweatshirt

Dirty and disheveled
She stood there
helpless

I rarely see females on their own
When I do they aren't asking for help
Instead keeping to themselves

The dog eat dog atmosphere

That is bred on the streets
Made me empathize with her
More than men

I dug into my change drawer
and found
Little Lincolns
Larger Jeffersons
Smaller Roosevelts
& quarter-sized Washingtons

As I placed them in her hand
She smiled from ear to ear
and a thank you thundered
From her chest

I contemplated my actions
As I filled up my tank.
Then I popped onto the 101 before she exited
From the convenience store
wondering what she wanted the money for

Calling on the Community

Change starts at the local level
Change starts with each of us

Are you willing to help your neighbor?
Not only the man or woman living next door
But neighbor like any person in your local grocery store
Or anyone that's inside or posted up in front of the post office.
Help has many faces and can look different for each of us
But establishing a willingness to assist is step one

If you answered yes
then the next step is *how*

We'll get to that

If you answered no
Well, you've taken the first step in creating a barrier within your
community. Division doesn't make for progress.
With more answers like that
communities will struggle with deep poverty for the foreseeable
future

Once we've each answered the question
It's time for a town meeting with elected officials.
Include a moderator
Then begin the brainstorm.
This is where we get to the *how* in *helping*

Caution: brainstorms take time and are known to be messy-
Especially since there are no simple solutions to alleviating poverty.
The overall goal is to generate plausible ideas
Grounded in practicality and compassion

Not everything that's said will stick, and that's ok

For the moderator, they must keep
The back and forth of opinions balanced

Because like a classroom discussion
When one voice rules them all, ideas will fall flat
and people will pop out of the dialogue
Because their voice has been silenced.

Speaking of voices
If we're going to come up with a solution for the community
Then everyone's voice must be heard
That means the homeless,
Those just above or below the poverty line,
The middle class, all the way to the millionaires
Need to be there because
If we want to improve our public spaces
We need the public to be present

If there are too many people that show up
THAT'S A GOOD PROBLEM TO HAVE
Split 'em up
Find community members that your elected officials trust
to adequately moderate conversation and then
put people in groups.
Let the locals get to know each other

With the topic of poverty
There will be pushback-
Not everyone will agree.
For those who disapprove,
they must propose an alternative solution.
The moderator will collect suggestions
and relay them back to elected officials

They are the ones who make the final decision
They are the ones who know the finances of the city or town
They are the ones who were elected to make choices on behalf of
everyone in the community
Then we vote on our options
That's democracy

Without knowing the solutions proposed by cities and towns,
I can say with certainty that it will involve sacrifice.

I have hope for humanity
After the Thomas Fire ravaged Ventura and Santa Barbara Counties
There was so much positive and nurturing energy going towards
those that were new to the homeless scene.
People knew they were one-bad-jump-of-the-flame from
losing everything.
Survivor's guilt was strong among people in the community;
It was a form of empathy.
If we can transfer those feelings and let our love loose on the
homeless, realizing that we are all closer to the streets than we
think, then we can put a human-centered approach to this urgent
humanitarian crisis.

Let's focus on affordable housing
Let's hold hospitals responsible
for adequate and accessible mental health care
Let's fund advocacy groups that provide support for families and
individuals who end up, or are close to, homelessness

We have to reimagine and reestablish what community means
We have to address income inequality in the ballot box and hold
our elected officials accountable
We have to ask whether or not having a place to call home is a
fundamental human right

The problem of deep poverty is real out here
And it's a problem that needs empathy as part of the equation
There are questions that need compassion as part of the solution
This epidemic needs the brightest minds,
The innovators
the ones transforming society through technology
To help us change how we interact with each other.

There is no problem too big for us to solve
From San Diego to Seattle
From Los Angeles to New York
Let's roll up our sleeves
Let's open our hearts
Let's put our minds together to

Create a community that we are all proud to call home,
An inclusive collection of individuals banded together
By the belief that accessible and affordable housing should be available to all

An American dream
That should be a reality

The Giver and The Taker

It started when he sat next to me

At a Starbucks by City Hall
He busted through my creative sound bubble
with eye contact,
Then he started his story

[taps the *pause* button]
Before I share his narrative
I'd be willing to bet
You've all heard a version of his story
You've all been asked to *spare some change*
You've all been asked for food or water
We've all listened to tales
With some being stronger than others,
Some more realistic
Some too basic

It all boils down to how people ask for help
and how much we can give of ourselves

It seems so simple
Someone asks for a little bit of assistance
We say *sorry I can't,* or pretend we didn't hear, and
keep moving
Or we stop and give what we can

But no matter how hard we try
We can't save everyone
We can't constantly give

Which brings us to Wharton's top-rated professor, Adam Grant

Grant gave us three categories
which we fulfill in social interactions

The *taker*
Who helps strategically- getting more than they give

The *giver*
Who gives more than they get- paying attention to what people
need

The *matcher*
Who balances giving with taking- aware of what's fair

When it comes to homelessness
The matchers are at bay
While the *givers* and *takers* are on full display

Strolling around major cities
We're constantly presented the opportunity
to play the role of *giver.*
With so many people asking for help,
We watch for *takers*
Both on the sidewalk and walking beside us
Trying our best to detect
The needy from the greedy.
In order to decipher this, the *giver* must
Quickly size up the situation.
Study the sign sitting before them, stop and listen to his/her story.
Decisions are made in seconds,
Since most of us are always on the move.

We help the man whose hand is out
Only to pass the next with nothing left to give
There are too many people
Again reminding ourselves that we can't save everyone
This makes the *giver* more selective,
which is depleting for both
The seeker of help
and the one seeking to help.
It's sad
It's disheartening
Since there are so many struggling on the streets
The only comfort for this is to

hope that there are more *givers* out there,
hope that our community is comprised of people wanting to help,
not knowing when we'll need the same from a stranger.
It's the golden rule in action.

Scratch the story that I started at the top
You've heard that story
But here's one you might not have heard
One that highlights what we hope our society can be:

In Philly
Off I-95
A young girl runs out of gas.
Dangerous neighborhood
The man sitting with his sign on the corner
Tells her to get back in her car and lock the doors
Floored, she sees him return with a gas can
He spent his last $20 to help her
A stranger in need.
He's our *giver*.
The girl, another *giver*, gave a gift
in the form of a GoFundMe page that told this story for all to read.
People responded by *giving* over $300,000
to help this man get back on his feet
which proved Pennsylvania's top professor's point:

Giving gives us all an opportunity to succeed
Giving creates compassionate communities

What can you give?

Resources

Below are a variety of resources that can be utilized to learn more about poverty across the United States.

Book   *Evicted: Poverty and Profit in the American City* by Matthew Desmond won the 2017 Pulitzer Prize Winner in General Nonfiction. After the economic crash in 2008, Desmond followed eight families in Milwaukee and documented how they managed to keep a roof over their heads. Extremely detailed, *Evicted* is the most comprehensive piece of literature I've read on poverty.

Movie   Directed by Sean Baker, *The Florida Project* tells the story of poverty on the outskirts of Disney World. Baker's film is different from other projects in the sense that his focuses on childhood. Funny, heartbreaking, and realistic, *The Florida Project* is a must-see for anyone looking to understand how poverty takes root from a young age.

Newspaper   *Los Angeles Times* journalists Gale Holland and Steve Lopez passionately provide in-depth coverage on poverty and homelessness in not only Los Angeles, but across Southern California.

Website   Philip Alston researched and analyzed the connection between civil rights and extreme poverty in the United States. Alston is the United Nations special rapporteur on extreme poverty and human rights. Alston's findings are comprehensive; if you want to understand what poverty looks like in America, and why economic inequality has persisted, this is a must-read.

Website   Homeless.lacounty.gov shares how tax dollars will be spent to help the nation's largest homeless population. Over the next five years, this website will be a case study for how a city with a major humanitarian crisis responds and uses public funds to help those who are living on the margins of society.

Website   Depending on where you live, a simple Google search can be a powerful tool for identifying and helping your local homeless shelter(s).

Acknowledgements

To my mother and father, for always encouraging me as both a teacher and writer. Your unwavering support is something I cherish.

To all of the poets in the Ventura community, with a special thank-you to Phil Taggart and Friday Gretchen for consistently hosting open mics at the E.P. Foster Library.

To my first creative writing partner, Sehar Kamal. We made a pact to write a book a few years back- and we both followed through. Your friendship, editing skills, and ability to hold nothing back made me a better writer. This book would not have been possible without you.

To Anna Walsh Palencia for your friendship, encouragement, and always available editing skills. I am forever grateful for your wisdom.

To all my friends in Ventura who listened and engaged with me regarding poverty and people. I know the topics weren't always alluring, but I appreciate you allowing me to explore my passions and curiosities.

To Dave Goldhahn for your creative vision on how to illustrate *Not So Simple*. Your flexibility and friendship throughout this entire process is something I truly valued.

To Mayo Morley and Richard La Plante, for guiding this young writer through the self-publishing process.

To my students for your enthusiasm to actively make a change in the community. Your eagerness and trust allowed me to be creative with class projects which in turn helped me develop a human-centered curriculum around communication and compassion.

About the Author

Brian Galetto is a poet and writer from South Jersey who currently lives in Ventura, CA.

He runs a website titled HappyFridayEveryDay.com that includes photography, prose, and poetry all focused on social justice issues and community activism.

He has taught communication, speech, English, and creative writing.

This is his first full-length collection of poems.

Made in the USA
San Bernardino, CA
22 October 2018